Dropshipping Success Blueprint: Mastering Product Sourcing

Introduction

Welcome to "Dropshipping: Product Sourcing," your essential guide to building and scaling a successful dropshipping business. In this book, I will share insights into sourcing suppliers across four distinct categories:

1. **General Sourcing**: Discover platforms that offer a wide range of suppliers and automation tools to streamline your operations.
2. **Niche Suppliers and Private Labeling**: Learn how to find specialized suppliers to cater to specific markets, stand out with unique product offerings, and create your own brand identity through private labeling.
3. **Print on Demand (POD)**: Understand the advantages of this innovative business model, allowing you to create and sell custom-designed products without inventory risks.

Whether you're a beginner or an experienced entrepreneur, this book will provide you with practical tips and resources and provide the best suppliers for your dropshipping journey. Let's dive in!

1: General Sourcing

Finding reliable suppliers is one of the fundamental aspects of running a successful dropshipping business. Luckily, general sourcing has been simplified through platforms that curate a wide selection of decent suppliers. These platforms save you time by eliminating the need to independently search for and evaluate the trustworthiness of individual suppliers.

The biggest advantage of using a dropshipping platform is its automation. Most platforms offer seamless integration with major eCommerce platforms like Shopify, WooCommerce, and Amazon. This integration streamlines the process of product listing, inventory management, and order fulfillment, allowing you to focus on scaling your business.

Moreover, many of these platforms provide training programs to help beginners navigate the complexities of dropshipping, making it an ideal starting point for new entrepreneurs.

Comprehensive Supplier Directories for General Sourcing.

1. AliExpress

AliExpress is a globally renowned marketplace connecting dropshippers to a vast network of suppliers, primarily from China. It serves as a convenient platform for beginners and experienced sellers alike, offering competitive pricing and a diverse range of products.

Shipping Locations
Ships to over 220 countries, including the US. Standard shipping takes 15-45 business days, while premium shipping options can deliver orders within 7-15 business days.

Product Selection
Boasts an impressive inventory of over 100 million products. Categories include fashion, electronics, toys, skincare, jewelry, furniture, and automotive parts.

Recommended For
Ideal for dropshippers seeking cost-effective sourcing and extensive product variety. A popular choice for market research and building supplier relationships.

---

2. AutoDS

AutoDS is a powerful dropshipping automation tool that integrates product sourcing, competitor analysis, and order fulfillment into one platform. It's particularly suited for scaling eCommerce businesses.

Shipping Locations
Leverages suppliers with warehouses in the US, UK, China, and Australia, ensuring global shipping options.

Product Selection
Offers access to over 500 million products from trusted suppliers

like Amazon, eBay, and AliExpress. Its in-app marketplace features daily updates with trending products.

Recommended For
Dropshippers focused on advanced tools for real-time bestseller analysis and automated operations.

---

3. DSers

DSers simplifies the connection between online stores and AliExpress suppliers. It enhances operational efficiency with its Supplier Optimizer feature, enabling users to compare and select the best suppliers for their needs.

Shipping Locations
Matches AliExpress's extensive shipping network, delivering to hundreds of countries worldwide.

Product Selection
Accesses AliExpress's vast catalog while providing insights into supplier performance and product quality.

Recommended For
Ecommerce store owners seeking to optimize supplier selection and streamline order processing.

---

4. Wholesale2B

Wholesale2B specializes in connecting dropshippers with USA-based suppliers, making it an excellent choice for domestic sellers.

Features

- Competitive wholesale prices.
- Seamless integrations with Shopify, WooCommerce, Magento, and other platforms.
- Alerts for price changes to help maintain profitability.

Pricing
Plans range from $37.99/month to $49.99/month depending on platform integration.

Recommended For
Dropshippers exploring USA suppliers who value easy integration and detailed pricing updates.

---

5. Worldwide Brands

Established in 1999, Worldwide Brands provides a certified directory of reliable wholesalers and dropshipping suppliers.

Shipping Locations
Supports global shipping, though costs and delivery times vary by supplier.

Product Selection
Offers access to over 16 million wholesale products across niches such as pet supplies, jewelry, electronics, home décor, and apparel.

Pricing
Lifetime membership available for a one-time fee of $299.

Recommended For
Retailers looking for high-quality, vetted suppliers and lifetime directory access.

6. CJDropshipping

CJDropshipping provides a comprehensive suite of services, including product sourcing, order fulfillment, and fast shipping.

Key Features

- Fast shipping options (2-3 days).
- Product and packaging customization services.
- Integration with Shopify, WooCommerce, and other platforms.

Recommended For
Dropshippers seeking a one-stop solution for managing orders and shipping in the US and beyond.

---

7. Zendrop

Zendrop specializes in seamless dropshipping for Shopify users, focusing on fast shipping and product customization.

Shipping Locations
Ships worldwide, with warehouses in the US and China.

Product Selection
Offers over a million products across categories, including automotive, baby items, clothing, and electronics.

Pricing
Free plan available; premium plans start at $49/month.

Recommended For
Shopify users looking for branded and customized product options with expedited delivery.

---

8. SaleHoo

SaleHoo is a trusted directory that connects sellers with over 8,000 verified suppliers, primarily catering to eBay and Amazon sellers.

Shipping Locations
Serves key markets in the US, UK, Australia, and New Zealand.

Product Selection
Features a broad range of products with seamless Shopify integration for added convenience.

Pricing
Starts at $27/month with a 30-day money-back guarantee.

Recommended For
Sellers seeking a reliable supplier directory with robust research tools.

---

9. Modalyst

Modalyst focuses on offering unique and high-ticket products, including luxury and trendy brands, for dropshipping stores.

Shipping Locations
Ships to over 80 countries. Domestic orders in the US are typically delivered in 5-8 days.

Product Selection
Specializes in curated, high-value items, including private label options.

Recommended For
Stores aiming to feature branded or premium products.

10. Spocket

Spocket connects retailers with global suppliers, emphasizing fast shipping and high-quality products.

Features

- Product samples and branded invoicing.
- Integration with Shopify, WooCommerce, and other platforms.
- Pricing plans starting at $39.99/month.

Recommended For
Retailers prioritizing quality and fast shipping for their customers.

11. Doba

Doba simplifies supplier connections, providing centralized management for dropshipping operations.

Shipping Locations
Supports global shipping, with rates varying by supplier.

Product Selection
Features over 2 million products across a diverse range of categories.

Pricing
Starts at $24.99/month.

Recommended For
Dropshippers seeking a streamlined platform for supplier management and product discovery.

12. Wholesale Central

Wholesale Central is a free directory that features numerous US-based dropshipping suppliers.

Shipping Locations
Primarily focuses on US-based suppliers, with varying shipping times.

Product Selection
Covers popular categories such as apparel, beauty products, and electronics.

Recommended For
Retailers looking for a free resource to find reliable suppliers.

---

13. Sellvia

Sellvia is known for its US-based dropshipping model with exceptionally fast delivery times.

Product Selection
Offers a curated catalog featuring trending items in niches like fashion, gadgets, and home goods.

Pricing
Monthly plans start at $39, while the yearly plan costs $299.

Recommended For
Dropshippers targeting US customers with high-quality products and fast shipping.

---

14. Dropified

Dropified streamlines sourcing and order fulfillment from platforms like Amazon, eBay, and AliExpress.

Features

- Bulk importing and automated order fulfillment.
- Comprehensive product research and review importing tools.

Pricing
Plans start at $19/month.

Recommended For
Dropshippers seeking efficient product management and streamlined operations.

---

15. Inventory Source

Inventory Source excels in automating supplier integrations and streamlining inventory management.

Features

- Syncs suppliers and products to eCommerce stores.
- Automates order placement and tracking updates.

Pricing
Free directory access; automation plans start at $99/month.

Recommended For
Retailers prioritizing automation and operational efficiency.

---

16. DropCommerce

DropCommerce is focused on high-quality products from US and Canadian brands, catering to premium retailers.

Features

- Product samples and branded invoices.
- Integration with Shopify, BigCommerce, and Wix.

Pricing
Starts at $19/month.

Recommended For
Retailers looking for high-quality, recognizable brands.

---

17. Sunrise Wholesale

Sunrise Wholesale offers an array of products from reputable brands such as Apple and Sony, ideal for high-value product categories.

Features

- Integration with major platforms like Shopify, eBay, Amazon, and BigCommerce.
- Daily inventory updates to ensure accuracy.

Pricing
$49/month.

Recommended For
Retailers targeting high-quality branded products for discerning customers.

18. BryBelly

BryBelly provides dropshippers with affordable, high-quality goods sourced from overseas manufacturers.

Features

- Flexible 45-day return policy with no restocking fees.
- Manual order processing for precise inventory control.

Pricing
Free.

Recommended For
Retailers prioritizing affordability and quality over automation.

---

19. EPROLO

EPROLO is a dropshipping platform that provides a one-stop solution for eCommerce stores.

Features

- Services include product sourcing, custom packaging, shipping, and tracking.
- Users can find, edit, and import products, and earn recurring commissions.

Compatibility
Compatible with Shopify, WooCommerce, and eBay.

Apps
Offers a Shopify dropshipping app, a free WordPress plugin, and a Chrome extension for adding products from AliExpress.

Cost
Free to register with no upfront costs.

Refund Policy
Full refunds for orders canceled before shipping, with exceptions for customized products and branding projects.

Reviews
Praised for its user-friendly interface, reliability, and streamlined processes. It is considered one of the best Shopify dropshipping suppliers.

Recommended For
Retailers looking for an alternative to AliExpress with robust tools and features.

---

20. DropshippingXL

DropshippingXL provides access to over 90,000 vidaXL products to customers across Europe, Australia, Japan, Canada, the USA, and the UAE.

Features

- Offers in-house production and a variety of brands.
- Manages inventory, shipping, returns, and customer support.
- Subscription at just €30/month.

Product Selection
Wide range of products, including furniture, garden supplies, tools, and more.

Recommended For
Retailers seeking a streamlined, all-inclusive platform for selling high-quality products globally.

Tips for Working with Dropshipping Suppliers (General Sourcing)

1. **Research Supplier Reputation**
   - Check reviews, testimonials, and ratings to ensure credibility.
   - Verify their operational history and ability to meet delivery timelines.
2. **Establish Clear Communication**
   - Use platforms like email, chat, or video calls to discuss terms and conditions.
   - Set clear expectations for quality, shipping times, and return policies.
3. **Request Product Samples**
   - Order samples to inspect the quality of products and packaging before listing them in your store.
4. **Negotiate Pricing and Terms**
   - Build relationships to negotiate better pricing, bulk discounts, or exclusive deals.
5. **Monitor Inventory Levels**
   - Work with suppliers that provide real-time inventory updates to avoid overselling.
6. **Start with Small Orders**
   - Test supplier reliability with small orders before scaling up.
7. **Use Automation Tools**
   - Leverage platforms like AutoDS or Inventory Source to manage inventory, orders, and tracking seamlessly.
8. **Understand Shipping Policies**
   - Review delivery times, shipping costs, and tracking options for different regions.
9. **Verify Return and Refund Policies**

- Ensure suppliers have clear policies for returns, exchanges, and refunds to maintain customer satisfaction.
10. **Stay Updated on Trends**
    - Collaborate with suppliers to identify trending products and gain insights into market demands.

Conclusion

Working with the right dropshipping supplier is the cornerstone of a successful eCommerce business. By leveraging the above directories and implementing best practices, you can streamline your operations, minimize risks, and maximize profitability. Stay proactive, build strong supplier relationships, and keep your focus on delivering value to your customers for long-term success.

2: Niche Suppliers and Private Labeling

When starting your dropshipping business, identifying and focusing on a niche is crucial. A well-defined niche not only helps you target specific customer groups but also differentiates your store in a competitive market. If you don't have any specific interests, consider exploring profitable niches recommended by industry leaders like Shopify and Forbes.

Niche Suppliers

Here's why niche suppliers are distinct from general suppliers or platforms:

- **Limited Automation**: Unlike general platforms, niche suppliers often require you to manually import products and

process orders. Most provide access through a simple login to their webpage, without the advanced automation tools offered by larger platforms.
- **Unique Product Offerings**: Niche suppliers give you access to exclusive and unique products that aren't widely available, helping you stand out in the market.
- **Cost-Effective**: Many niche suppliers don't charge membership fees, saving you a significant amount of money in the long run.

Private Labeling

Private labeling is an excellent way to establish a unique brand identity while leveraging existing manufacturing resources. In this model, products are manufactured by one company but sold under your brand. This approach gives you control over branding and pricing without the need to manage manufacturing.

Private labeling also simplifies logistics. The manufacturer not only produces the goods but also ships them directly to your customers on behalf of your brand. By adopting this strategy, you can:

- **Differentiate Your Brand**: Create exclusive products that align with your brand's vision and target audience.
- **Control Pricing**: Set competitive pricing strategies tailored to your market.
- **Focus on Marketing**: Concentrate your efforts on promoting your brand while the manufacturer handles production and shipping.

This combined strategy of niche suppliers and private labeling is ideal for entrepreneurs looking to build a sustainable brand with minimal overhead costs while catering to specific market demands.

We are dividing the suppliers into four categories: **Fashion**, **Beauty**, **Jewelry**, **Pet Products** and **Others**.

Fashion Suppliers

1. BrandsGateway

BrandsGateway specializes in high-end fashion dropshipping, offering luxury brands to retailers around the world. With warehouses located in Europe and the USA, including Italy and Germany, BrandsGateway provides fast dispatch times and exclusive access to designer clothing from top labels like Gucci and Prada.

- **Product range**: Designer clothing from brands like Gucci, Prada, and Dolce & Gabbana.
- **Shipping policies**: Fast dispatch times (24 hours) with delivery within the EU taking approximately 72 hours.
- **Unique features**: Membership fee required ($295/month); access to over 100 luxury brands and exclusive products; supports multiple currencies and languages for international sales.
- **Main characteristics**:
  - Extensive product catalog of more than 20,000 items from over 100 luxury brands including Dolce & Gabbana, Gucci, Galliano, Versace, Cavalli, Armani, Michael Kors, and many others.
  - Automated dropshipping available for stores based on Shopify, Wix, Shift4Shop, BigCommerce, and WooCommerce, as well as RestAPI integrations for custom-based stores.
  - Opportunity to sell luxury clothing and accessories with high margins of up to 250%.
  - Flexibility to expand reach by selling on platforms like Amazon and eBay.

- Convenient 14-day return policy.
- Accessible to customers in over 170 countries worldwide.
- Orders typically arrive within 1-7 working days.
- Marketing materials are available at no cost.

2. **WEIV**

Based in Los Angeles, WEIV is dedicated to providing high-quality non-branded men's clothing at affordable prices. The company focuses on creating stylish yet accessible apparel for everyday wear, catering primarily to the US market.

- **Product range**: Shirts, pants, hoodies, jackets, and more.
- **Shipping policies**: Domestic shipping within 3-5 business days; international shipping varies by location.
- **Unique features**: No minimum order quantity required; emphasis on customer service and high-quality products; simple inquiry process to access dropshipping services.
- **Dropshipping program**: Subscription-based, with monthly account fees. Partners with Syncio to ensure easy inventory and image sync (Syncio account required).

3. **Wholesale7**

Wholesale7 is an online dropshipping clothing supplier that provides a wide range of affordable men's fashion items. Possessing an extensive inventory that includes casual wear and formal attire, Wholesale7 caters to various retail needs.

- **Product range**: Casual wear, formal attire, accessories, and more.
- **Shipping policies**: Shipping times vary by location but generally offer efficient logistics for fast delivery.
- **Unique features**: Extensive product range with competitive pricing; regular updates to inventory to stay ahead of fashion trends; customization options for bulk orders.

4. Q Clothing

Q Clothing is a UK-based supplier recognized for its fashionable men's apparel at attractive prices. The dropshipping clothing supplier offers a variety of stylish clothing items, including discounted designer labels.

- **Product range**: A variety of stylish men's clothing including designer items at discounted rates.
- **Shipping policies**: Shipping times vary; VAT is not included in listed prices for UK orders.
- **Unique features**: Offers ex-chainstore products allowing access to designer labels at lower costs; flexible ordering options suitable for both small and large retailers.

5. Trendsi

Trendsi specializes in women's clothing, providing access to a wide variety of trendy apparel and accessories for dropshippers. The platform features dresses, tops, bottoms, and outerwear designed to meet the latest fashion demands.

- **Product range**: Dresses, tops, bottoms, and outerwear for women.
- **Shipping policies**: Domestic orders typically take 5-7 days for delivery.
- **Unique features**: Free membership with no upfront costs; branded invoices for a professional touch; training courses available for new dropshippers. Conducts quality inspections and ships every order from a US warehouse within 2-10 business days, all under the brand's invoice. Offers a 7-day free return policy for customers.

6. Silverts

Silverts has a long-standing history in the fashion industry, specializing in adaptive clothing that caters to seniors and people with disabilities.

- **Product range**: Adaptive clothing for seniors and individuals with disabilities.
- **Shipping policies**: Rapid shipping across North America.
- **Unique features**: Customization options; straightforward pricing structure with no setup fees; substantial discounts on bulk orders; occasional promotions and additional discounts for partners.

7. Tasha Apparel

Founded in 2014, Tasha Apparel is a dropship clothing supplier in Los Angeles offering a wide range of products for girls and women.

- **Product range**: Loungewear, swimwear, activewear, and more.
- **Shipping policies**: Same-day dispatch for orders placed before 12 pm PST; fast delivery within the US.
- **Unique features**: No restocking fee for returns within 7 days of purchase.

8. KidsBlanks

Kids Blanks is an excellent option for businesses looking for customizable clothing items for babies and children. Targeting basic apparel such as onesies, t-shirts, and rompers, they cater to businesses interested in personalizing products through print or embroidery. They are ideal for boutique owners and creative sellers.

- **Product range**: Blank clothing for all age groups, with customization services.
- **Shipping policies**: Quick turnarounds with orders dispatched within 1-2 business days; affordable international shipping options.
- **Unique features**: Offers screen printing and embroidery services; minimum order of 48 products for customization.

9. ModeShe

ModeShe is a Hong Kong-based dropshipping supplier offering stylish and modern clothing for women aged 18 to 35.

- **Product range**: Formal and casual wear for women.

- **Shipping policies**: Efficient logistics with flexible cancellation options.
- **Unique features**: No subscription fee; no MOQ (minimum order quantity); easy cancellations with a full refund for orders canceled within 12 hours.

10. BelleWholesale

BelleWholesale is a Chinese B2B online fashion dropshipper specializing in trendy women's clothing, footwear, and accessories. They feature twelve different brands, including Lily Apparel and Sporty Space. BelleWholesale regularly updates its inventory to reflect the latest global trends, making them ideal for fashion-conscious audiences.

- **Order discounts**: Dropshippers get an additional 5% discount on every order.
- **Lenient return policy**: You can make a return request within 14 days of receipt.

11. Matterhorn Wholesale

Matterhorn Wholesale is a Poland-based wholesaler that dropships women's clothing, lingerie, footwear, and accessories. Known for its European finesse, Matterhorn Wholesale provides stylish collections suited for formal and casual settings. They sell more than 27,000 products from brands like Amour, Numoco, and FIGL.

- **Automated orders**: You can either place orders manually on the Matterhorn Wholesale website or automatically through their API.

- **High quality**: Matterhorn Wholesale has good quality products and is reliable in terms of service.
- **Shipping costs**: Shipping anywhere outside Europe starts at €12.
- **Slow delivery**: Delivery outside Europe takes seven to ten business days.
- **Return policy**: Only accepts returns for damaged products.

---

12. Coco-Fashion

Coco-Fashion is a dropshipping supplier based in Poland that sells women's and men's clothing from European designers. Their elegant, high-quality streetwear fashion items include dresses, tops, blouses, and jackets.

- **New styles**: Offers around 20 new styles weekly.
- **Size inclusivity**: Includes standard and plus-size styles.
- **Return policy**: Accepts returns within 14 days from the delivery date.

---

13. Niceshop

Niceshop is an emerging fashion supplier focusing on trendy women's clothing with a broad appeal to younger demographics.

- **Product range**: Dresses, activewear, and casual styles.

- **Shipping policies**: Offers international shipping with delivery within 7–15 days.
- **Unique features**: No minimum order requirements; regular discounts for dropshippers; user-friendly platform for order tracking.

---

14. FashionTIY

FashionTIY offers a versatile range of apparel for both women and men, making it a go-to platform for businesses seeking variety.

- **Product range**: Women's and men's clothing, accessories, and footwear.
- **Shipping policies**: Supports fast shipping to global destinations.
- **Unique features**: Competitive pricing with bulk discounts; frequent inventory updates to keep up with trends.

---

15. Infant Wear Bambini

Infant Wear Bambini specializes in baby clothing made from sustainable materials like cotton. Their focus on eco-friendly practices appeals to environmentally-conscious consumers seeking quality babywear and accessories. With reliable customer service and flexible return policies, this supplier stands out in the baby clothing market.

- **Product range:** Cotton babywear, blankets, and accessories.
- **Shipping policies:** Ships worldwide from California; shipping costs depend on package weight/size.

- **Unique features:** Focus on eco-friendly materials; accepts returns within 7 days of delivery with options for refunds or store credit; reliable customer service.

---

16. Annloren

Location: USA
Niche: Children's clothing and accessories
AnnLoren is a US-based dropshipping supplier that offers a selection of clothing sets, dresses, rompers, shirts, and shorts for kids aged 3 months to 14 years.

- **Product range:** Clothing and accessories for girls and boys.
- **Return policy:** Accepts returns and refunds in the form of payment if the order is sent back within 14 days. If an order is returned within 21 days, the available option for refund is store credit.

---

17. Your New Style

Location: Poland
Niche: Clothing
Based in Poland, Your New Style is a dropshipping supplier of women's and men's clothing that sources its products mostly from France, Italy, and England.

- **Product range:** Sells women's and men's clothing.

- **Dropshipping program:** Offers integration for Shopify, Magento, WooCommerce, or Prestashop.
- **Shipping:** Provides shipping to Europe, Russia, the USA, Asia, and Africa with DPD, GLS, or Post.

---

18. Buy2Bee

Location: Italy
Niche: Clothing and accessories
Buy2Bee is an Italy-based dropshipping company with two warehouses that cover worldwide delivery of their products.

- **Product range:** Sells clothing and accessories for women, men, and kids.
- **Shipping policies:** Shipping costs vary by package weight and destination country.
- **Returns:** Accepts returns only for items in their original condition that haven't been worn.

---

19. Siatex

Location: Bangladesh
Niche: Kids' clothing
Siatex is a leading dropshipping supplier of kids' clothing based in Bangladesh, with over 36 years of experience in the wholesale industry. The company offers a diverse range of children's apparel, including t-shirts, hoodies, dresses, onesies, and pajamas.

- **Product range:** A variety of baby clothes including onesies and sleepwear.
- **Shipping policies:** Takes about one week to make sample products; bulk orders take approximately three weeks for production/shipping.
- **Unique features:** Offers private labeling and customization options; conducts multiple quality checks before shipping.

20. Micha Made in Italy

Location: Italy
Niche: Clothing and accessories
Micha Made in Italy is a manufacturing laboratory from Modena that produces various textiles for third parties. They are a well-established brand for women's clothing, offering garments up to size 50.

- **Dropshipping services:** Full service for dropshippers.

21. Katydid Wholesale

Location: USA
Niche: Women's clothing
Katydid Wholesale is both a wholesaler and dropshipping supplier of women's leisure and sportswear.

- **Shipping:** Takes around 1-3 days, slightly slower than other suppliers.
- **Return policy:** Strict, requiring product returns within 3 days from the delivery date.

22. Style Centre

Location: UK
Niche: Clothing and accessories
Style Centre is a UK dropshipping supplier that provides luxury fashion items for men. They focus on men's clothing and accessories and offer a well-organized support system for dropshippers.

- **Inventory:** Restocked and renewed weekly.
- **Return policy:** Only accepts returns for faulty and damaged items.

23. Ujena

Location: USA
Niche: Women's Swimwear
Ujena specializes in the niche market of dropshipping swimwear, including bikinis, tankinis, cover-ups, and summer dresses.

- **Shipping:** Orders are shipped and received within 12 business days regardless of location.
- **Inventory:** The company is always in stock.

24. Sweetlegs

Location: Canada
Niche: Activewear
Sweetlegs is a dropshipping clothing supplier from Canada,

focusing on activewear and leggings for women. They offer unique collections at low costs.

25. Male Basics

Location: USA
Niche: Men's underwear
Male Basics focuses on intimate clothing, menswear, swimwear, and sportswear. They provide promotional resources like product descriptions and 360-degree demonstrations.

26. Atixo

Location: Germany
Niche: Clothing
Atixo is a German dropshipping supplier specializing in unique clothing products like costumes, lingerie, and dirndls. Orders placed before 2 PM are shipped the same day.

27. Kiyonna

Location: USA
Niche: Plus-size Women's clothing
Kiyonna is a clothing supplier specializing in plus-size clothing for women. Orders are shipped within 24-48 hours after placement.

The fashion suppliers listed here offer a diverse range of products, from trendy fast-fashion items to luxurious high-end apparel, ensuring there's something for every style and market niche. With these reliable partners, your business can stay ahead of the trends and deliver quality, on-trend fashion to your customers.

Beauty & Cosmetics Suppliers

1. Nordstrom

A trusted name in the fashion business since 1901, Nordstrom offers a wide range of luxury cosmetics and apparel for dropshipping.

- **Key Features**: Free shipping and returns in most US regions. Global shipping through Borderfree with delivery in 5-13 business days.
- **Brands Offered**: Bobbi Brown, CHANEL, Dior, Estee Lauder, MAC.
- **Product Categories**: Makeup, skincare, beauty tools.
- **Payment Methods**: Credit cards, Nordstrom gift cards, Apple Pay, Google Pay.

---

2. DR. HC

Specializing in organic, vegan, and natural cosmetics, DR. HC offers a comprehensive dropshipping program with private labeling options.

- **Key Features**: Low membership costs ($39.99 or $59.99), no minimum order quantity (MOQ), fast order processing (1-3 working days).

- **Supported Platforms**: Shopify, WooCommerce, Squarespace, and more.
- **Product Categories**: Skincare, makeup, hair & body care, bath items.

---

3. Beauty Joint

A US-based distributor offering affordable dropshipping programs for cosmetics in various categories.

- **Key Features**: One-time setup fee ($25) + $15/month subscription. Multiple global shipping options, including USPS.
- **Brands Offered**: Loreal, NYX, LA Girl.
- **Product Categories**: Makeup, body care, skincare, haircare.

4. CoLour Zone

A UK-based supplier offering cosmetics and more, with quick dispatch and international shipping options.

- **Key Features**: Orders dispatched within 2 days. Wide product catalog, including perfumes and trendy dresses.
- **Product Categories**: Makeup (eyes, lips, face), nail care, skincare.

5. *Blanka – POD Cosmetics*

Blanka is a North American-based supplier that specializes in private-label cosmetics dropshipping, making it easy to create and sell your branded products.

- **Key Features**: No minimum order quantity (MOQ), 14-day free trial, and affordable monthly plans starting at $29 (Growth Plan), $59 (Scale Plan), and $99 (VIP Plan).
- **Manufacturing Location**: North America.
- **Product Categories**: Vegan and cruelty-free makeup, skincare, beauty tools, and high-quality formulations for eyes, lips, and face.
- **Platforms Supported**: Seamlessly integrates with Shopify and other eCommerce platforms.

6. Strawberry

Based in Hong Kong, Strawberry offers an extensive range of cosmetics and beauty products with international shipping.

- **Key Features**: Over 800 brands and 33,000 products at wholesale prices. Supports most international credit cards for payments.
- **Product Categories**: Makeup, skincare, haircare, perfumes, natural beauty products.

7. *Viaglamour*

A Canadian dropshipping supplier specializing in natural, vegan, and cruelty-free cosmetics with private-label branding.

- **Key Features**: Custom packaging, flat $4.99 shipping within the US, and integration with Shopify for streamlined order management.
- **Shipping Coverage**: Canada, US, Australia, France, and other global locations.
- **Product Categories**: Makeup, skincare, beauty tools.

8. Greendropship

A US-based supplier focusing on natural, organic, and handmade beauty products with no minimum order requirements.

- **Key Features**: Supports Shopify, WooCommerce, and marketplace merchants. Shipping via USPS and FedEx, including frozen and refrigerated products.
- **Product Categories**: Organic makeup, skincare, and natural beauty items.

9. Zosmetic

A leading Korean beauty dropshipping supplier offering branded cosmetics at competitive prices.

- **Key Features**: Skin analysis technology for product recommendations, quick order processing (1-4 working days).
- **Brands Offered**: The Face Shop, Bio Miracle, Accoje, and more.
- **Shipping**: Domestic shipping within India and international delivery via trusted couriers.
- **Product Categories**: Korean skincare, makeup, and beauty tools.

10. BTSwholesaler

A European supplier providing a broad range of branded cosmetics and sun care products for dropshipping within the EU.

- **Key Features**: Branding services with products shipped under your logo, support for multiple languages across EU countries.
- **Brands Offered**: Dior, Estee Lauder, and other top brands.
- **Product Categories**: Makeup, sun care, and beauty products.

11. Viatrading

A family-owned wholesale company in Los Angeles offering discounted and liquidation cosmetics for dropshipping.

- **Key Features**: No MOQ or licensing requirements, bulk ordering options available.
- **Product Categories**: Discounted cosmetics, pre-packaged beauty products.

12. Jubilee

Jubilee specializes in supporting entrepreneurs in the U.S. and Canada to create private-label beauty brands with a focus on quality and flexibility. With tailored solutions for emerging businesses, Jubilee is a trusted partner for launching cosmetic lines.

- **Key Features**: Private-label packaging, sample ordering at wholesale costs, and no minimum order quantity (MOQ).
- **Shipping Policies**: Flexible ordering options with an average delivery time of 4-9 business days.
- **Product Categories**: Skincare, makeup, and beauty products.

---

13. FragranceNet

FragranceNet is a popular supplier of perfumes, skincare, haircare products, and aromatherapy items. They also offer candles and cosmetics from luxury brands like Versace, Givenchy, and more. With a vast selection of over 17,000 products, FragranceNet ensures high-quality offerings for eCommerce sellers targeting the beauty and lifestyle niches.

- **Shipping:** Starts at $6.95 for orders under $59; free shipping on orders over $59.
- **Unique features:** No membership fees, regular promotional discounts, and seasonal stock updates.
- **Product range:** Fragrances, skincare products, haircare, aromatherapy oils, and candles.

---

14. Born Pretty

Born Pretty is a trusted dropshipping supplier specializing in nail care products. Their catalog includes a wide range of nail products from top brands and their own private-label offerings.

- **Key Features**: Offers products from brands like Nee Jolie and UR Sugar, along with Born Pretty's private-label items. Provides access to a dropshipper discount once approved.

- **Shipping Policies**: International shipping with warehouses in the US and UK; orders fulfilled within 3-7 days.
- **Product Categories**: Nail polish, nail powder, nail decorations, UV gel polishing lamps, and more.

Pros:

- Wide range of products.
- Major brand partnerships.
- International shipping.

Cons:

- Possibility of application rejection.

15. Beauty Big Bang

Beauty Big Bang offers a variety of dropshipping options, including nail care, personal care, and makeup products. Its program is open to all merchants and is easy to implement.

- **Key Features**: Free international shipping, diverse product range, and a simple process for listing and shipping.
- **Shipping Policies**: Free international shipping (terms and conditions apply).
- **Product Categories**: Nail care (polishes, decorations, stamping plates), makeup (eyeliner, kits, brushes), and personal care products.

Pros:

- Wide range of products.
- Free international shipping.

Cons:

- Variable wholesale pricing.

---

16. Dermacol Cosmetics

Dermacol Cosmetics offers its own-brand beauty products with a focus on quality and innovation, including cannabis-based products. They provide both a wholesale and dropshipping program.

- **Key Features**: Exclusive access to Dermacol products with options for direct delivery and email support.
- **Shipping Policies**: Products ship directly from Dermacol; details provided upon partnership.
- **Product Categories**: Hair care, skincare, body care (exfoliation, hair removal, muscle balms), and beauty accessories.

Pros:

- Direct delivery.
- Access to a wholesale program.
- Unique product formulations.

Cons:

- Limited to Dermacol-branded products.

---

17. SheaByNature

SheaByNature specializes in authentic shea butter products and offers a rigorous dropshipping program to ensure high-quality partnerships.

- **Key Features**: Partners receive a 25% discount on retail prices, and products are made from genuine shea butter.
- **Shipping Policies**: Delivers to the UK and Europe; manual inventory and import processes.
- **Product Categories**: Skin creams, face creams, soaps, and lip balms.

Pros:

- Authentic products.
- 25% discount on retail prices.
- Delivery within Europe and the UK.

Cons:

- Manual inventory and import processes.

18. BeautéTrade

BeautéTrade is a global marketplace that connects businesses with vetted suppliers of beauty products, making it ideal for creating a diverse product catalog.

- **Key Features**: Free account creation, access to reliable suppliers, and marketing functionalities to enhance store visibility.
- **Shipping Policies**: Dependent on the selected supplier; must contact suppliers directly for dropshipping options.
- **Product Categories**: Organic beauty products, skincare, makeup, and more.

Pros:

- Wide range of products.
- Free account creation.

- Verified and reliable suppliers.

Cons:

- No direct integration with eCommerce platforms.

The beauty and cosmetics section offers a curated selection of reliable suppliers, ensuring high-quality products, diverse options, and seamless dropshipping solutions to help you create and scale your beauty brand with confidence.

Jewelry Suppliers

1. CheapWholesaleJewelry

CheapWholesaleJewelry offers a variety of jewelry items, from necklaces and rings to earrings and bracelets. Their catalog caters to trendy and affordable jewelry buyers, ensuring a wide audience for eCommerce stores.

- **Dropshipping requirements:** $129.95 one-time fee.
- **Discounts:** 10% discount for dropshippers.
- **Shipping:** Free domestic shipping for orders above $50.
- **Unique features:** White-label service for private branding.

2. **Richard Cannon Jewelry**

Richard Cannon Jewelry specializes in fine jewelry, offering elegant and luxurious items like rings, necklaces, and bracelets. Their products are ideal for sellers targeting a premium market.

- **Product range:** Over 3,000 SKUs in fine jewelry.
- **Shipping:** Worldwide delivery within 5–7 days.
- **Unique features:** High-quality craftsmanship and exclusive designs.

3. **Pierce Body**

Pierce Body is a leading supplier of body jewelry, offering an extensive catalog of items like earrings, nose rings, and belly button rings. Their products are affordable and cater to a younger audience.

- **Shipping:** Free shipping for orders above $500.
- **Product categories:** Piercing kits, stainless steel jewelry, and body adornments.

4. **Topearl**

Topearl focuses on pearl-based jewelry, offering timeless and elegant designs. Their high-quality craftsmanship makes them an attractive supplier for the luxury fashion market.

- **Shipping:** Delivery within 10–20 days globally.
- **Dropshipping benefits:** Free dropshipping with unbranded packages.

- **Product range:** Pearl necklaces, earrings, and bracelets.

---

5. Nihaojewelry

Nihaojewelry specializes in trendy, affordable fashion jewelry. Their collections are frequently updated to reflect current styles, making them ideal for fast-fashion jewelry sellers.

- **Integration:** Compatible with Shopify for easy product listing.
- **Shipping:** 3–15 days via ePacket.
- **Unique features:** Competitive pricing and a large catalog.

---

6. oNecklace

oNecklace offers customizable jewelry options, allowing customers to personalize items like necklaces, bracelets, and rings with engravings or initials.

- **Shipping:** 5–10 days delivery within the US.
- **Unique features:** Focused on personalized designs with quality craftsmanship.

---

7. SilverBene

SilverBene specializes in 925 sterling silver jewelry. They cater to high-quality jewelry markets with timeless designs.

- **Dropshipping benefits:** Free dropshipping services and a 30-day return policy.
- **Product range:** Sterling silver necklaces, rings, and earrings.

8. MMA Silver

MMA Silver provides a vast collection of sterling silver jewelry, focusing on timeless, elegant pieces. Their products cater to premium markets.

- **Dropshipping benefits:** Free dropshipping and support with marketing materials.
- **Product range:** Over 4,000 sterling silver items.

9. US Jewelry House

US Jewelry House offers a mix of high-quality and affordable jewelry items, ideal for boutique retailers and online sellers.

- **Product range:** Rings, necklaces, bracelets, and more.
- **Dropshipping benefits:** Bulk discounts available.
- **Shipping:** Ships across the US.

10. Gold N Diamonds

Gold N Diamonds is a supplier of fine, customizable jewelry. Their collections include wedding bands, engagement rings, and anniversary pieces.

- **Unique features:** High-quality craftsmanship with an emphasis on customization.
- **Shipping:** Free shipping; delivery typically within a week.

11. Nihao Jewelry

Nihao Jewelry is a top-rated supplier for jewelry dropshipping, offering an extensive range of fashion accessories. Their collections include earrings, necklaces, bracelets, rings, and more, catering to diverse styles and trends. They focus on providing high-quality and budget-friendly products, ensuring accessibility for small businesses and new sellers entering the market.

- **Product range:** Fashion accessories including earrings, necklaces, bracelets, and rings.
- **Unique features:** No minimum order requirements and frequent inventory updates.
- **Shipping policies:** Worldwide shipping available; delivery times depend on the destination.
- **Additional benefits:** Affordable prices suitable for small businesses.

12. JewelryBund

JewelryBund is a Chinese supplier specializing in bulk jewelry and fashion accessories. They provide a variety of trendy products, making them ideal for budget-conscious dropshippers. Their products often feature contemporary designs catering to a wide customer base.

- **Product range:** Earrings, bracelets, necklaces, and accessories.
- **Shipping policies:** Global shipping with options for expedited delivery.
- **Unique features:** Offers custom designs for bulk orders.
- **Return policy:** 14-day return policy for defective items.

13. PinkTown USA

PinkTown USA is an American jewelry supplier that focuses on trendy and urban-style accessories. They cater to businesses targeting a youthful demographic and frequently update their inventory with the latest fashion trends to meet market demands.

- **Product range:** Statement jewelry, chokers, layered necklaces, and earrings.
- **Shipping policies:** Ships within 1–2 business days; free shipping available for orders over $100.
- **Unique features:** Regular updates to collections.
- **Return policy:** Returns accepted within 7 days of delivery.

14. Alamode Fashion Jewelry

Alamode Fashion Jewelry is a reliable supplier offering high-quality, wholesale jewelry with a focus on contemporary designs. Their dedication to quality makes them a preferred choice for dropshippers looking to provide premium items.

- **Product range:** Rings, necklaces, earrings, bracelets, and other fashion jewelry.
- **Shipping policies:** Ships worldwide with competitive rates.
- **Unique features:** Offers private labeling services for dropshippers.
- **Return policy:** Returns accepted within 15 days of receipt.

15. Silverbene

Silverbene specializes in sterling silver jewelry and offers a wide variety of elegant designs suitable for premium markets. Their expertise in fine craftsmanship ensures products of excellent quality.

- **Product range:** Sterling silver necklaces, earrings, rings, and bracelets.
- **Shipping policies:** Worldwide shipping with tracking; free shipping on bulk orders.
- **Unique features:** Custom designs and engraving services.
- **Return policy:** Returns accepted within 30 days for unused items.

16. Fashion Bella

Fashion Bella is a California-based wholesale jewelry supplier providing a broad collection of affordable and trendy accessories. Their platform is well-suited for new sellers and those with smaller budgets.

- **Product range:** Earrings, rings, bracelets, necklaces, and hair accessories.
- **Shipping policies:** Domestic shipping within 1–3 business days; international shipping available.
- **Unique features:** No minimum order requirements.
- **Return policy:** Returns accepted within 7 days of delivery.

17. DDFL Import

DDFL Import specializes in fashion and costume jewelry for businesses looking to target customers with affordable yet stylish products. They focus on offering a variety of designs to suit different tastes.

- **Product range:** Costume jewelry, rings, necklaces, and bracelets.
- **Shipping policies:** Ships within 2–3 business days; international shipping available.
- **Unique features:** Offers discounts on bulk orders.
- **Return policy:** 14-day return policy for defective items.

18. WeSilver Jewelry

WeSilver Jewelry is a Thailand-based supplier known for its handcrafted sterling silver jewelry. They cater to premium and mid-range markets with a focus on high-quality products.

- **Product range:** Sterling silver earrings, necklaces, rings, and bracelets.
- **Shipping policies:** Ships globally with fast delivery options.
- **Unique features:** Customizable jewelry designs and engraving options.
- **Return policy:** 30-day return policy for unused items.

19. Ruby Imports

Ruby Imports is a wholesale jewelry supplier offering a variety of fashionable items at competitive prices. They are particularly suited for businesses aiming to provide affordable yet attractive products.

- **Product range:** Earrings, bracelets, necklaces, and other accessories.
- **Shipping policies:** Domestic shipping within the USA and international shipping options.
- **Unique features:** No minimum order requirements.
- **Return policy:** Returns accepted within 7 days for defective products.

20. Gemologica

Gemologica specializes in gemstone jewelry, offering an elegant selection of rings, pendants, and bracelets. Their premium products are ideal for sellers targeting customers looking for unique and high-quality gemstone pieces.

- **Product range:** Gemstone rings, pendants, and bracelets.
- **Shipping policies:** Worldwide shipping with tracking.
- **Unique features:** Custom gemstone settings.
- **Return policy:** Returns accepted within 30 days for unused items.

21. Wholesale Sparkle

Wholesale Sparkle is a leading supplier of sterling silver and cubic zirconia jewelry, offering a mix of classic and modern styles. Their products are ideal for sellers who want to target both traditional and contemporary markets.

- **Product range:** Sterling silver and cubic zirconia rings, earrings, necklaces, and bracelets.
- **Shipping policies:** Fast shipping within the USA and international delivery available.
- **Unique features:** Discounts for bulk purchases.
- **Return policy:** Returns accepted within 14 days for unused items.

The jewelry suppliers listed above offer a diverse range of options suitable for different market needs, from affordable costume pieces to premium sterling silver and gemstone collections. By partnering with these suppliers, dropshippers can effectively meet their customers' demands for high-quality and stylish jewelry.

Pet Products Suppliers

1. PetStoresUSA

- **Best For**: Retailers seeking an extensive variety of pet products from a trusted supplier with a strong industry presence.
- **Location**: Centrally located in Cincinnati, Ohio, ensuring timely nationwide delivery.
- **Products Offered**:

- Pet toys
- Accessories
- Grooming tools
- Health and wellness items

MOQ: No minimum order quantity (MOQ), accommodating businesses of all sizes.

Key Features:

- Broad selection of over 2,500 products.
- Exclusive wholesale distributorship to avoid direct retail competition.
- Knowledgeable account representatives.

Pros:

- Expansive product catalog.
- No competing retail sales.
- Central warehouse for efficient shipping.

Cons:

- Limited international shipping options.
- Requires partnership and account setup.
  Pricing: Contact their team directly for pricing and partnership agreements.

2. TopDawg

- **Best For**: E-commerce businesses of all sizes looking for an extensive catalog with easy integration into e-commerce platforms.
- **Location**: Network of suppliers across the United States.
- **Products Offered**:
    - Pet supplies (dogs, cats, etc.)

- Home decor
- Fashion and accessories

MOQ: No minimum order quantity.

Key Features:

- Catalog of over 700,000 products.
- Seamless integration with leading e-commerce platforms.
- Advanced API for efficient order management.

Pros:

- Extensive product selection.
- No upfront costs with a free account option.
- Global dropshipping capabilities.

Cons:

- Overwhelming product options may take time to navigate.
- Higher-tier plans required for advanced features.

Pricing:

- START-UP: Free (limited features).
- BUSINESS: $19.99/month.
- SCALE: $44.99/month.

---

3. Mirage Pet Products

- **Best For**: Dropshippers looking for a diverse range of pet attire and accessories, including American-made products.
- **Location**: Southwest Missouri, ensuring efficient US shipping.
- **Products Offered**:
    - Dog and cat apparel

- Crystal collars
- Pet hoodies
- Pet toys

MOQ: Flexible MOQ policy.

Key Features:

- Nearly 70 years of industry experience.
- American-made products.
- Customization options available.

Pros:

- High-quality, fashionable pet products.
- Fast US shipping.
- Diverse product range.

Cons:

- Higher pricing due to US manufacturing.
- Limited international shipping.

Pricing: Contact Mirage Pet Products directly for pricing.

---

4. Essential Pet Products

- **Best For**: Online retailers looking to dive into the pet industry without the need to stock inventory.
- **Location**: United States.
- **Products Offered**:
    - Dog and cat toys
    - Pet clothing
    - High-tech pet gadgets

- Fashion-forward accessories

MOQ: No minimum order quantity.

Key Features:

- No inventory required.
- Access to top-selling brands.
- Data feeds and marketing support.

Pros:

- Vast selection of quality products.
- Resources for business growth.
- Focus on trending items.

Cons:

- Primarily serves the US market.
- Requires becoming an Authorized Retailer.

Pricing: Contact for pricing details; competitive rates offered.

---

5. Pet Supply UK

- **Best For**: Dropshippers targeting the UK market, particularly those focusing on racing pigeons.
- **Location**: United Kingdom.
- **Products Offered**:
    - Pigeon foods and treatments
    - Dog food and treats
    - Pigeon care accessories

MOQ: Flexible MOQ policy.

Key Features:

- Specialized pigeon care products.
- Competitive pricing.

Pros:

- Niche specialization.
- Reliable for pigeon enthusiasts.

Cons:

- Limited appeal beyond pigeon products.
- UK-focused services.

Pricing: Contact directly for pricing and details.

---

6. HyperSKU

- **Best For**: Shopify sellers and direct-to-consumer brands seeking efficient dropshipping and fulfillment services.
- **Location**: Fulfillment centers in China and the US.
- **Products Offered**:
    - Pet supplies (costumes, collars, toys)
    - Customized packaging and private label products

MOQ: No minimum order quantity.

Key Features:

- Sourcing on demand (quotes within 48 hours).
- Private labeling and custom packaging.
- One-click product import.
- Express shipping (7-12 days).

Pros:

- Direct factory sourcing ensures competitive pricing.

- Simplified fulfillment process.
- Localized online support.

Cons:

- Mainly tailored for Shopify sellers.
- Dependency on HyperSKU for sourcing.

Pricing: No upfront fees or memberships; pay only for fulfilled orders.

---

7. Gor Pets

- **Best For**: Dropshippers focusing on premium comfort-centric pet products.
- **Location**: Details not provided.
- **Products Offered**:
    - Pet beds and cushions
    - Durable pet toys
    - Stylish accessories

MOQ: Not disclosed.

Key Features:

- Comfort-focused pet products.
- Easy-to-navigate website.

Pros:

- High-quality, pet-friendly products.
- Customer favorites.

Cons:

- Limited transparency on location and MOQ.

Pricing: Contact Gor Pets for detailed pricing.

---

8. The Paws

- **Best For**: Dropshippers with a focus on socially responsible and eco-friendly pet products.
- **Location**: Bali, Indonesia.
- **Products Offered**:
    - Eco-friendly pet accessories
    - Pet apparel
    - Innovative pet toys

MOQ: No minimum order quantity.

Key Features:

- Socially responsible business model.
- Island-inspired designs.
- Portion of proceeds supports dog welfare.

Pros:

- Supports animal welfare initiatives.
- Unique product range.

Cons:

- Limited to dog products.
- Location may affect shipping times.

Pricing: Contact for pricing details; competitive rates provided.

9. Pet Wholesale USA

- **Best For**: Independent retailers seeking a vast selection of pet products, including aquarium and reptile supplies.
- **Location**: United States.
- **Products Offered**:
  - Aquarium supplies
  - Reptile essentials
  - General pet care items
  - Grooming products

MOQ: Varies by product.

Key Features:

- Over 10,000 products from 200+ brands.
- User-friendly website with Wishlist and Quick Order tools.
- Reliable dropshipping services.

Pros:

- Family-owned business with consistent service.
- Extensive product range.
- Competitive wholesale pricing.

Cons:

- US-only service.
- Business account required for purchasing.

Pricing: Contact for pricing and details.

10. Central Pet

- **Best For**: Dropshippers seeking a wide range of pet products and strategic partnerships for business growth.
- **Location**: Distribution centers across the United States.
- **Products Offered**:
  - Elanco products
  - Benebone dog chews
  - Farmland Traditions dog treats
  - Greenies™ smart nutrition dog food

MOQ: Varies by product.

Key Features:

- Products from 300+ vendor partners.
- Regular portfolio updates.
- Customer experience teams for support.

Pros:

- Largest assortment of pet products.
- Visibility for vendors to thousands of retailers.

Cons:

- Overwhelming product range for smaller dropshippers.

Pricing: Contact Central Pet for tailored pricing details.

---

11. ZooDrop

- **Best For**: E-commerce businesses, eBay sellers, and breeders seeking a comprehensive range of pet supplies in Germany.
- **Location**: Germany.

- **Products Offered**:
    - Dog and cat accessories
    - Pet food
    - Small pet supplies
    - Bird accessories

MOQ: No minimum order quantity.

Key Features:

- Marketing materials and product images included.
- Streamlined product integration.
- Handles logistics and postage.

Pros:

- Extensive range of high-quality pet products.
- No need for inventory or logistics.

Cons:

- Shipping restricted to Germany.
- Pricing visible only after registration.

Pricing: Flat shipping fee of €5.99 net within Germany (taxes additional).

---

12. A Pet's World

- **Best For**: Retailers and dropshippers catering to fashion-conscious pet owners.
- **Location**: United States.
- **Products Offered**:

- Designer dog clothing
- Fashionable pet totes
- Personalized pet accessories

MOQ: Contact directly for MOQ details.

Key Features:

- Hand-sewn embellishments.
- Personalized products.
- Updated seasonal designs.

Pros:

- High-quality, fashion-forward designs.
- Customization options available.

Cons:

- Higher pricing due to designer focus.
- Limited selection for non-designer products.

Pricing: Contact for wholesale and dropshipping fees.

---

13. K9 Bytes

- **Best For**: Dropshippers seeking niche, handmade pet items.
- **Location**: United States.
- **Products Offered**:
    - Handmade treats for dogs and cats
    - Handcrafted collars, leashes, and toys

MOQ: Details available upon inquiry.

Key Features:

- Locally produced, high-quality items.
- Colorful and unique designs.

Pros:

- Appeals to customers seeking handmade products.
- High-quality craftsmanship.

Cons:

- Limited product range.

Pricing: Contact directly for details.

---

14. Majestic Pet Products

- **Best For**: Dropshippers looking for a diverse range of pet products, including custom items.
- **Location**: San Antonio, Texas, USA.
- **Products Offered**:
    - Custom pet beds
    - Cat trees
    - Dog crates

MOQ: Not explicitly listed.

Key Features:

- Long-standing reputation.
- Customizable products.

Pros:

- High-quality product variety.

- Customization options.

Cons:

- Limited information on MOQ.

Pricing: Contact for tailored pricing.

---

15. Go Pet Club

- **Best For**: Retailers focusing on stylish and durable pet products.
- **Location**: United States.
- **Products Offered**:
    - Cat trees and condos
    - Pet beds and strollers

MOQ: No minimum order quantity.

Key Features:

- Non-toxic, eco-friendly materials.
- Free shipping.

Pros:

- Stylish, high-quality products.
- No MOQ.

Cons:

- Limited to furniture and accessories.

Pricing: Pricing varies based on product type.

---

16. Iconic Pet

- **Best For**: Dropshippers prioritizing high-quality, durable pet products.
- **Location**: United States.
- **Products Offered**:
    - Luxury pet furniture
    - Engaging toys
    - Playpens and cages

MOQ: Low MOQ.

Key Features:

- Safety-focused, premium products.
- Durable designs.

Pros:

- High-quality items.
- Diverse product range.

Cons:

- Premium pricing.

Pricing: Available upon inquiry.

Choosing the right supplier is a critical step in building a successful pet product business. Each of the suppliers listed here offers unique advantages, whether it's an extensive product catalog, niche offerings, or eco-friendly practices. As a dropshipper, consider factors like shipping options, product quality, and MOQ requirements to find the best fit for your business. By partnering with reliable suppliers, you can focus on growing your brand and providing exceptional value to your customers, ensuring long-term success in the thriving pet market.

Other Suppliers

1. **GreenDropShip**

GreenDropShip focuses on natural, organic, and eco-friendly products. It offers an extensive catalog of over 20,000 items sourced from 800 US-based brands. This supplier caters to a wide variety of niches, including health, beauty, food, and household items.

- **Membership:** $149/year.
- **Integration:** Compatible with Shopify, WooCommerce, Amazon, and eBay.
- **Shipping:** Fast delivery across the US through three warehouse locations.
- **Product categories:** Organic snacks, skincare products, eco-friendly household items, and more.

2. **Furniture Pipeline**

Furniture Pipeline offers lightweight, eco-friendly, and sustainable furniture. Their products are designed for modern and minimalistic homes, with options for customization and white labeling.

- **Product range:** Desks, shelves, tables, and seating.
- **Shipping:** Quick delivery across the US.
- **Unique features:** SEO-friendly product listings for online stores.

3. **Sagebrook Home**

Sagebrook Home provides a wide array of home decor products, including lighting, furniture, and wall art. Their high-end inventory caters to interior designers and decor enthusiasts.

- **Product range:** Over 10,000 items, including vases, lamps, mirrors, and furniture.
- **Dropshipping requirements:** Requires a verified business website for account approval.
- **Shipping:** Ships primarily within the US.

4. # MegaGoods

MegaGoods is a US-based supplier specializing in consumer electronics, gadgets, and kitchen appliances. They offer competitive pricing and a wide selection of products.

- **Membership:** No upfront fees; a $1.50 fee is charged per order.
- **Shipping:** Ships domestically within the US.
- **Product range:** Home electronics, kitchen gadgets, and gaming accessories.

5. # Banggood

Banggood is a Chinese dropshipping giant that provides a variety of products ranging from electronics and gadgets to apparel and home goods. They cater to global audiences and offer multilingual support for sellers.

- **Membership:** Free access to dropshipping tools.
- **Shipping:** ePacket and express shipping options for global orders.
- **Unique features:** Personalized recommendations and VIP discounts for high-performing dropshippers.

6. Auchan

Auchan is a dropshipping app for online stores dealing in French products. It sources products from leading French manufacturers and offers thousands of SKUs across various categories. Auchan ensures that all products are kept under optimum conditions based on French legislation criteria, guaranteeing durable, high-quality products for customers.

- **Highlight Features:**
    - Specializes in sourcing French products from leading manufacturers.
    - Products kept under optimum conditions based on French legislation criteria.
    - Diverse product catalog ranging from kids' toys to skincare and more.
- **Suitable for:**
    - Entrepreneurs seeking genuine French products.
    - Those interested in exploring a free plan to access the catalog.

7. CROV

CROV connects retailers to a wide range of products from a vetted list of US dropshipping wholesalers covering various industries. A unique feature of CROV is its product request feature, allowing merchants to reach out to CROV's professional sourcing team for supplier recommendations based on their business's unique needs.

- **Highlight Features:**
    - Product Request Feature: Merchants can request supplier recommendations from CROV's professional sourcing team.

- Wide Range of Products: CROV offers over 35,000 products in over 20 trending categories.
- US Warehouse: Faster domestic shipping with a US-based warehouse for selected products.
- **Suitable for:** Ecommerce sellers seeking various products for platforms like Shopify, Amazon, and eBay.
- **Based in:** US

8. PlusBuyer

PlusBuyer is a dropshipping supplier that specializes in electronic products from top manufacturers. It's a place where you can find all these goods at cheap wholesale prices. PlusBuyer offers dropshipping services to its registered customers at no extra charge. Note that there is no official connector that can sync data between the two platforms. You either have to do everything manually or rely on third-party apps.

- **Best for:** Unique selection of products not available on other platforms.

9. Bedding Dropship

Bedding Dropship is a New Jersey–based dropshipping supplier dedicated to providing duvet covers, bedding sets, window treatments, and other small bed and bath home goods and accessories.

- **Best for:** Dropshipping bedding and small bed and bath furniture accessories.
- **Shipping:** Within three days for fast delivery, with automated tracking updates.
- **Returns:** Unused items accepted for return up to 30 days after the purchase date.

- **Requirements:** $25 application fee (credited to the first order) and a valid business tax ID.

10. DHgate

DHgate is another China-based marketplace for dropshipping products across a wide range of niches. It's known for affordability, but merchants should be cautious about product quality—always read reviews.

- **Best for:** Sourcing affordable dropshipped furniture with buyer protection.
- **Product categories:** Outdoor furniture, home furniture, commercial furniture, other furniture, furniture accessories, children's furniture, baby furniture.
- **Fees:** No signup or monthly fees.

11. Dropshipzone

Dropshipzone is an Australia-based marketplace where merchants can find dropshippers and wholesalers to source products.

- **Best for:** Australia-based merchants.
- **Product categories:** Bar stools and chairs, bathroom, bedroom, dining, living room, mattresses, office, sofas, outdoor furniture.
- **Unique features:** Easy side-by-side product comparison.

12. Fast Furnishings

Fast Furnishings is a US-based online marketplace dedicated to selling furniture and related home goods. It facilitates both B2C and B2B sales through its Wholesale Drop-Ship Reseller Program.

- **Best for:** Sourcing high-quality dropshipped furniture from industry experts.
- **Product catalog:** Over 3,000 products.
- **Shipping:** Free shipping within the contiguous US.
- **Membership:** Pro plan available for $49/month or $39/month (billed annually) with additional benefits.

13. GFURN

GFURN is a Canada-based furniture, lighting, and home décor accessories supplier offering direct-to-consumer sales, wholesale, and dropshipping.

- **Best for:** US- and Canada-based merchants seeking high-quality furniture.
- **Shipping:** Daily outgoing shipments with no order minimums.
- **Discounts:** Discounted container pricing for large wholesale orders.

14. VIG Furniture

VIG Furniture is a Los Angeles–based furniture wholesaler and dropshipper specializing in high-quality furniture, with thousands of products for merchants to choose from.

- **Best for:** Dropshipping high-quality, design-forward furniture in the contiguous US.
- **Shipping:** Most orders delivered within a week.
- **Unique features:** No minimum purchase amount or application fees.

15. Wholesale Interiors

Wholesale Interiors specializes in home and commercial furniture items for dropshipping.

- **Best for:** Sourcing high-quality home and commercial furniture items.
- **Product categories:** Dining room furniture, bedroom furniture, home office furniture, lighting, outdoor furniture, living room furniture, entryway furniture, and more.
- **Requirements:** Free application and documentation showing business registration.
- **Branding:** Uses its own branding, "Baxton Studio," on boxes, but not on receipts or labels.

16. Artisan Furniture US

Artisan Furniture US specializes in handcrafted, solid wood furniture that brings a unique, high-quality touch to any space.

- **Best for:** Dropshipping solid wood furniture.
- **Advantages:** No minimum order requirements and free delivery across all 50 states.
- **Customization:** Customers can choose from various stains, paint finishes, and fabrics.

17. Blessed Bean Coffee

Blessed Bean Coffee is a wholesaler based in Florida. It dropships a wide variety of products, such as single-origin beans, flavored coffees, and decaf beans. While custom brews are not available, their online store offers a rich selection of roasts, blends, flavors, and origins.

- **Specialty:** High-quality coffee blends and flavors.
- **Product range:** Single-origin beans, flavored coffees, and decaf options.
- **Location:** Based in Florida, USA.

18. **Old Chicago Coffee Co.**

Old Chicago Coffee Co. is a US-based dropshipping coffee supplier known for its global coffee varieties and customizable packaging. They offer the ability to brand the packaging with your logo and a range of blends, grinds, and bag sizes—including K-Cup style capsules.

- **Specialty:** Customizable packaging and premium coffee varieties.
- **Product range:** Blends, grinds, bag sizes, and single-serve K-Cup capsules.
- **Shipping:** Free domestic shipping within the USA.

19. **Dripshipper**

Dripshipper is a Shopify app that simplifies starting an online coffee business. Their dropshipping service automatically prepares and ships coffee and tea products as soon as orders are received. The packaging is branded with your logo for a personalized touch.

- **Platform:** Shopify-integrated dropshipping app.
- **Turnaround time:** Orders shipped within 3-5 days.
- **Unique feature:** Automated processes and private-label branding.

20. **Temecula Coffee Roasters**

Temecula Coffee Roasters is a low-barrier entry coffee supplier with flexible order sizes and no membership fees. They offer private-label support, including logo design, product photography, and app integration with online stores.

- **Specialty:** Private-label support and flexible order sizes.

- **Fees:** No membership fees.
- **Additional services:** Branding, photography, and app integration.

21. Aroma Ridge Coffee Roasters

Georgia-based Aroma Ridge Coffee Roasters provides signature blends and flavored coffees as white-label products. They also allow merchants to create unique private-label blends tailored to their brand identity.

- **Specialty:** White-label and private-label coffee products.
- **Startup fee:** $100 one-time fee.
- **Product range:** Signature blends, flavored coffees, and private-label options.

The suppliers listed above represent a diverse array of niches and product categories, catering to businesses of all types and sizes. Whether you're looking to specialize in eco-friendly goods, cutting-edge electronics, or premium coffee, these suppliers offer robust solutions to meet your dropshipping needs. Each supplier provides distinct advantages, such as flexible shipping options, private-label opportunities, and tools to integrate seamlessly with popular eCommerce platforms.

3: **Print on Demand (POD)**

Print on demand (POD) is a popular dropshipping model that offers flexibility and low upfront costs. With POD, products are created only after an order is placed. Items like t-shirts, mugs, posters, and books are designed by sellers and printed by third-party services.

This model is particularly appealing for those who want to test different designs or product ideas without committing to large inventory investments. Key benefits of POD include:

- **No Inventory Management**: Products are printed, packed, and shipped directly by the service provider, freeing you from inventory concerns.
- **Creative Freedom**: Experiment with a variety of designs and product categories, such as apparel, accessories, and home decor.
- **Low Risk**: Since products are made to order, you avoid the financial risk of unsold inventory.

Ready to get started? Leverage free training, intuitive tools, and dedicated support to build, run, and grow your t-shirt business or expand into other product categories. The print-on-demand model is an excellent opportunity to combine creativity with entrepreneurship.

Top Print-on-Demand Suppliers for Dropshipping Success

1. Printful

Printful is a leading name in the global print-on-demand (POD) industry, known for its reliability and quality. The company operates fulfillment centers in the USA, Mexico, and Europe, ensuring fast delivery and excellent service.

Key Features:

- Offers 200+ customizable products, including clothing, homeware, stationery, artwork, and accessories.
- Provides a user-friendly mockup generator for creating designs.
- Multiple printing options available, such as sublimation and embroidery.
- Custom branding options like tags, stickers, and inserts to enhance your brand identity.
- Products are typically ready to ship within 2–5 days and delivered worldwide.
- Allows customers to personalize products via a free customization tool integrated into your store.

Integrations: Compatible with major eCommerce platforms, including Shopify, WooCommerce, BigCommerce, and Magento.

2. Printify

Printify is a POD platform offering a network of global suppliers for flexible product options and competitive pricing.

Key Features:

- Access to over 800+ customizable products, from apparel to pet accessories.
- Flexible pricing plans, including a free plan and premium subscriptions for discounts.
- Allows users to choose suppliers based on location and cost for faster shipping.
- Automated order processing and fulfillment.

Integrations: Compatible with Shopify, Etsy, WooCommerce, eBay, and more.

3. SPOD

SPOD is known for its fast production times and user-friendly design tools.

Key Features:

- Over 100 customizable products, including apparel, mugs, and tote bags.
- 48-hour production guarantee for most orders.
- Built-in design tools for creating unique products easily.
- Eco-friendly options and sustainable packaging available.

Integrations: Compatible with Shopify, WooCommerce, and Etsy.

4. Teespring (Spring)

Teespring is a creator-focused platform for designing and selling custom merchandise.

Key Features:

- Wide range of products, from apparel to digital items.
- Integrated storefronts for creators to showcase their collections.
- Built-in marketing tools and integrations with social platforms.

Integrations: Direct integration with YouTube, Instagram, and Twitch.

---

5. Gooten

Gooten is a scalable print-on-demand platform ideal for businesses of all sizes.

Key Features:

- Offers 150+ customizable products, including home decor and wall art.
- Enterprise-level tools for automation and bulk order processing.
- Network of global suppliers for efficient fulfillment.

Integrations: Compatible with Shopify, WooCommerce, Etsy, and custom APIs.

6. Apliiq

Apliiq specializes in premium custom apparel with advanced branding options.

Key Features:

- Focus on apparel, including custom tags, labels, and packaging.
- Small-batch crafting with high attention to detail.
- Direct embroidery and screen printing options available.

Integrations: Compatible with Shopify and WooCommerce.

---

7. Redbubble

Redbubble is an artist-driven marketplace offering products featuring unique, independent designs.

Key Features:

- Wide range of products like apparel, stickers, and home decor.
- No upfront costs or inventory management required.
- Artists earn commissions from sales on the platform.

Integrations: Operates as a self-contained platform.

---

8. Zazzle

Zazzle focuses on customizable products for personal and corporate use.

Key Features:

- Large catalog of items, from stationery to home decor.
- Robust design tools for customers and sellers.
- Ideal for personalized gifts and bulk orders.

Integrations: Operates as a self-contained marketplace.

9. T-Pop

T-Pop is an eco-friendly POD platform with sustainable products and packaging.

Key Features:

- Organic apparel and biodegradable packaging options.
- Carbon-neutral shipping to minimize environmental impact.
- Focus on ethical production practices.

Integrations: Compatible with Shopify, Etsy, and WooCommerce.

10. Gelato

Gelato is a global POD platform with local production in over 30 countries.

Key Features:

- Products include wall art, apparel, and stationery.
- Local fulfillment ensures faster shipping and reduced costs.
- Enterprise-level scalability for growing businesses.

Integrations: Compatible with Shopify, WooCommerce, and APIs.

11. CustomCat

CustomCat offers a wide selection of products and efficient order fulfillment.

Key Features:

- Over 350+ customizable items, including mugs, apparel, and wall art.
- Bulk discounts available for higher margins.
- Quick production turnaround.

Integrations: Compatible with Shopify, WooCommerce, and API access.

12. Society6

Society6 is an artist-focused POD platform offering unique designs on a variety of products.

Key Features:

- Large catalog, including art prints, furniture, and apparel.
- Artist-first platform where creators earn royalties.
- High-quality printing and premium materials.

Integrations: Operates as a self-contained platform.

13. Merch by Amazon

Merch by Amazon allows creators to sell custom apparel directly through Amazon.

Key Features:

- Access to Amazon's vast customer base.
- No upfront costs or inventory management.
- High-quality printing and fulfillment by Amazon.

Integrations: Operates exclusively on Amazon's marketplace.

14. Threadless

Threadless supports artists by providing a platform to sell designs on various products.

Key Features:

- Offers apparel, accessories, and home decor.
- Community-focused with promotional support for artists.
- Zero upfront costs or inventory requirements.

Integrations: Operates as a self-contained platform.

15. Fine Art America

Fine Art America is a POD platform tailored for artists and photographers.

Key Features:

- Products include canvas prints, apparel, and home decor.
- Tools for marketing and promoting artwork.
- High-quality printing with a focus on fine art.

Integrations: Integrates with Shopify and custom websites via APIs.

16. Kin Custom

Kin Custom offers fully customizable apparel and accessories with branding options.

Key Features:

- Custom packaging and labeling options available.
- Wide range of apparel and accessory products.
- Sustainable practices in production and packaging.

Integrations: Compatible with Shopify and Etsy.

17. Spreadshirt

Spreadshirt is a user-friendly platform for selling custom-designed merchandise.

Key Features:

- Wide product range, including apparel and accessories.
- Easy-to-use design tools for creating unique products.
- Allows sellers to set up their own online shops.

Integrations: Operates as a standalone platform.

18. Shirtee

Shirtee is a European POD platform with a focus on quality and sustainability.

Key Features:

- Eco-friendly production and packaging options.
- Fast delivery across Europe.
- Advanced customization tools for creating designs.

Integrations: Compatible with Shopify and WooCommerce.

---

19. Bella+Canvas

Bella+Canvas offers premium apparel for custom designs and branding.

Key Features:

- High-quality materials and eco-conscious manufacturing.
- Focus on trendy and comfortable apparel.
- Bulk order discounts for businesses.

Integrations: Works with various POD platforms for seamless fulfillment.

---

20. Print Aura

Print Aura is a versatile POD service with a wide range of customizable products.

Key Features:

- Offers over 200+ products, including apparel and home decor.
- No monthly fees or upfront costs.
- Custom branding options like labels and packaging inserts.

Integrations: Compatible with Shopify, Etsy, and WooCommerce.

21. Bonfire

Bonfire specializes in custom apparel campaigns for individuals and organizations.

Key Features:

- Focus on t-shirts, hoodies, and activewear.
- Ideal for fundraising and group campaigns.
- No upfront costs or inventory management required.

Integrations: Operates as a standalone platform.

22. T-Shirt Gang

T-Shirt Gang is a POD service focusing on quick setup and efficient fulfillment.

Key Features:

- Wide range of t-shirts and apparel items.
- Easy-to-use platform for sellers.
- Fast production and shipping times.

Integrations: Compatible with Shopify and WooCommerce.

23. Yoycol

Yoycol offers an extensive range of all-over print products.

Key Features:

- Specializes in full-print customization.
- Large product catalog, including apparel and accessories.
- Competitive pricing with no minimum order requirements.

Integrations: Compatible with Shopify, Etsy, and WooCommerce.

24. JetPrint

JetPrint focuses on print-on-demand watches and unique accessories.

Key Features:

- Offers a niche selection, including custom watches and footwear.
- Advanced 3D mockup generator.
- Quick production and global shipping.

Integrations: Compatible with Shopify and WooCommerce.

25. Inkthreadable

Inkthreadable is a UK-based POD service offering eco-friendly options.

Key Features:

- Organic and sustainable products available.
- Focus on ethical manufacturing practices.
- Wide product range, including clothing and homeware.

Integrations: Compatible with Shopify and WooCommerce.

With these suppliers, businesses of all sizes can find the ideal print-on-demand partner to bring their creative ideas to life. Whether your focus is on sustainability, niche products, or global scalability, this list offers a diverse array of options to suit any eCommerce strategy.

How To Find the Best Dropshipping Niches

What is a Dropshipping Niche?

A dropshipping niche is a specialized segment of a market that can be served by dropshipped products. Examples of potential niches include:

- Fitness gear
- Eco-friendly pet supplies
- Home office furniture

Dropshipping is a retail fulfillment method where a store doesn't stock its products. Instead, when a store makes a sale, it purchases the item from a third party, which ships it directly to the customer on the store's behalf.

Selecting a dropshipping niche allows you to focus your marketing efforts, differentiate your brand from competitors, and create a strong brand identity.

How to Find a Dropshipping Niche?

Businesses often succeed or fail based on how well they meet consumer demand. If nobody wants your product, you'll struggle to make sales. As the saying goes, it's easier to fill existing demand than to create it. Below are tips to help you identify the best niches:

1. Use Tools to Research Demand

Understanding a product's demand, competition, and suppliers is essential to making an informed decision. Thankfully, several online tools can help measure demand and identify top dropshipping niches:

Audience Insights

Meta's Audience Insights aggregates information about users on platforms like Facebook, Instagram, and WhatsApp. It helps determine the size of a potential niche and provides valuable demographic data.

Key insights include:

- **Demographics**: Age, gender, lifestyle, education, job role, and relationship status.
- **Page Likes**: Categories and topics of interest to your audience.
- **Location**: Where people live and the languages they speak.
- **Activity**: Ads clicked, comments made, promotions redeemed, devices used, and more.

For example, if you're exploring a niche like fitness and wellness, you can input keywords and see how many active monthly users are interested worldwide. Additionally, you can review their likes and geographic locations.

Google Keyword Planner

Google's Keyword Planner provides search volume data, allowing you to understand how many people are searching for specific terms each month.

Key Metrics:

1. **Match Type**: Use the exact-match option to get the most accurate search volume for a keyword.
2. **Search Location**: Distinguish between local search volume (specific to your target country or region) and global search volume. Focus on local results if you're targeting a specific market.

3. **Long-Tail Variations**: Longer, more specific keywords often represent the majority of search traffic. These detailed terms, known as long-tail keywords, indicate a deeper interest in a niche.

When analyzing potential markets, ensure the keyword has a variety of actively searched variations. If related search terms drop off quickly, the niche may lack depth.

Google Trends

Google Trends offers insights that Keyword Planner doesn't, such as search interest over time and regional popularity.

Features:

- **Search Interest Over Time**: Monitor whether the niche is growing or declining.
- **Top and Rising Terms**: Identify the most popular related searches and trending queries. These can guide your marketing and SEO efforts.
- **Geographic Concentration**: Discover where potential customers are concentrated geographically.
- **Seasonality**: Understand demand fluctuations throughout the year. Seasonal spikes can mislead conclusions if measured during peak or low periods.

2. Explore Online Marketplaces

Online marketplaces such as Amazon, eBay, Etsy, and AliExpress are great resources for discovering trending products.

Start by exploring the various categories or departments on the marketplace, such as electronics or home and garden. Identify trending or bestselling products, often highlighted in sections labeled as "Bestsellers" or "Hot Products." This can give you insight into what consumers are currently buying.

Use filters and sorting options to narrow down your search and explore product subcategories. The more subcategories you find, the deeper that niche may be. Check out the competition and analyze their pricing strategies to ensure there's room for a profitable markup. Look for niches with a balance between demand and manageable competition.

3. Look for Accessory-Heavy Niches

Customers tend to be less price-sensitive about accessories, allowing for larger markups. For example, while a customer may take weeks to compare prices for a TV, they might spend $30 on an HDMI cable without hesitation. Often, businesses earn higher profit margins on accessories than on big-ticket items.

By choosing a niche with lots of accessories, you can enjoy higher profit margins and attract less price-sensitive shoppers.

4. Find Customers with Passion

Passionate hobbyists are often willing to spend significant money on their interests. For example:

- Mountain bikers might invest heavily in lightweight accessories.
- Avid fishermen may spend thousands on boats and gear.

If you offer products that solve specific problems or enhance these hobbies, you'll find a loyal customer base eager to buy.

5. Look for Trendy Products You Can't Find Locally

Trendy products that are hard to find locally give you a competitive advantage. Customers searching online will be more likely to buy from you. However, ensure that the product also has ample demand to make the niche worthwhile.

6. Aim for Niches with Low Product Turnover

Frequent product changes can drain your resources and time. Opt for niches where product lines have limited turnover, allowing you to build a consistent and information-rich website that remains viable for years.

7. Consider Selling Consumable or Disposable Products

Repeat customers are key to long-term success. Consumable or disposable products that require regular reordering can create a steady stream of recurring revenue. By keeping your customers happy, you'll foster loyalty and enjoy repeat sales.

8. Evaluate Profit Margins

Before committing to a niche, calculate your potential profit margins. Dropshipping involves various costs, such as supplier fees, shipping charges, and marketing expenses. A niche with low-profit margins might not be worth pursuing, even if the demand is high.

- **Cost Analysis**: Compare the wholesale price from suppliers to the retail price consumers are willing to pay.
- **Shipping Costs**: Factor in whether shipping fees might eat into your profits. Some niches, like lightweight or compact items, naturally have lower shipping costs.

- **Return Policies**: High return rates can reduce profitability, so choose products that are less likely to be returned due to defects or sizing issues.

9. Test Your Niche with Minimal Risk

Rather than diving headfirst into a niche, validate your ideas with small-scale testing. You can:

- Run low-budget ad campaigns targeting your potential audience.
- List a few products on marketplaces like eBay or Etsy to gauge interest.
- Use pre-order models to measure demand before investing in inventory or additional marketing.

Testing allows you to refine your approach and minimize risks before fully committing.

10. Stay Adaptable

Trends and consumer preferences can change quickly, especially in the dropshipping industry. Stay informed about new developments in your niche and be prepared to pivot if necessary. Tools like Google Alerts, social media monitoring, and industry newsletters can help you keep track of emerging trends and consumer behaviors.

Examples of Profitable Dropshipping Niches

To inspire your journey, here are some niches with proven profitability:

1. **Eco-Friendly and Sustainable Products**
   Rising consumer awareness about environmental issues has boosted demand for products like reusable water bottles, biodegradable bags, and solar-powered gadgets.
2. **Pet Care and Accessories**
   Pet owners are willing to splurge on their furry friends. Popular items include luxury pet beds, interactive toys, and custom pet apparel.
3. **Health and Wellness**
   Products like yoga mats, resistance bands, and organic supplements cater to the growing trend of personal health improvement.
4. **Home Office Essentials**
   With the rise of remote work, ergonomic furniture, desk organizers, and noise-canceling headphones are in demand.
5. **Hobby and Craft Supplies**
   Passionate hobbyists often invest in specialized tools, kits, or materials for activities like painting, knitting, and woodworking.

Avoiding Common Pitfalls in Niche Selection

Selecting the right niche is crucial, but there are common mistakes to avoid:

1. **Ignoring Competition**
   While competition isn't inherently bad, entering an oversaturated market can make it hard to stand out. Focus on niches where you can add unique value.
2. **Overlooking Supplier Reliability**
   Partnering with unreliable suppliers can lead to delays, poor

product quality, and dissatisfied customers. Always vet potential suppliers thoroughly.
3. **Choosing a Niche Without Longevity**
Fads can fade quickly, leaving you with unsold inventory and wasted resources. Aim for niches with long-term demand.

Action Plan

To start your dropshipping journey:

1. Use tools like Google Keyword Planner, Google Trends, and Audience Insights to shortlist potential niches.
2. Validate your niche by testing products on platforms like Etsy or running small ad campaigns.
3. Focus on building a strong brand identity and customer trust by offering high-quality products and excellent service.

With diligent research and a clear strategy, you can create a successful dropshipping business that stands out in your chosen niche.

Long-Term Strategies for Dropshipping Success

While finding the right niche is critical, maintaining and scaling your dropshipping business requires a proactive approach to several key areas:

Build a Strong Brand

Even in a competitive niche, a strong brand can differentiate your business and foster customer loyalty. Focus on:

- **Professional Design**: Invest in a visually appealing website and cohesive branding, including your logo, color scheme, and packaging.
- **Clear Messaging**: Clearly communicate your brand's mission and values. For instance, if you're focusing on eco-friendly products, highlight sustainability in your messaging.
- **Customer Experience**: Offer fast, responsive customer service to address queries and resolve issues quickly.

Master Digital Marketing

Effective marketing is the backbone of a successful dropshipping business. Utilize the following strategies:

- **Social Media Marketing**: Leverage platforms like Instagram, TikTok, and Pinterest for visually-driven niches such as fashion or home décor.
- **Content Marketing**: Publish blogs, videos, or infographics that provide value to your audience. For instance, if your niche is fitness gear, create workout tutorials or fitness tips.
- **Email Campaigns**: Build an email list and send regular updates, product promotions, and content to nurture customer relationships.
- **Paid Ads**: Run targeted ad campaigns on platforms like Google Ads, Facebook Ads, or TikTok Ads. Start with small budgets to test ad performance and scale successful campaigns.

Prioritize Customer Retention

Acquiring new customers is more expensive than retaining existing ones. Encourage repeat purchases by:

- Offering loyalty programs with discounts or rewards for repeat customers.

- Sending personalized recommendations or exclusive deals based on past purchases.
- Using subscription models for consumable products, such as monthly shipments of skincare or coffee.

Optimize Operations

Efficient operations are crucial for scaling. Focus on:

- **Automation**: Use tools like Oberlo, Spocket, or Zendrop to streamline order processing and inventory management.
- **Supplier Relations**: Build strong partnerships with reliable suppliers to ensure quality and timely delivery.
- **Analytics**: Regularly review key metrics like conversion rates, cart abandonment, and customer lifetime value to identify areas for improvement.

Expanding into Global Markets

Once you've established a foothold in your local market, consider expanding internationally. Key steps include:

1. **Localized Marketing**: Adapt your website, ads, and product descriptions to suit different languages and cultures.
2. **Currency Options**: Allow customers to pay in their local currency to simplify transactions.
3. **International Shipping**: Partner with logistics providers who specialize in global fulfillment to ensure smooth delivery.

Popular International Dropshipping Niches

Some niches have universal appeal, including:

- Fashion and accessories
- Beauty and skincare

- Consumer electronics
- Baby products

Leveraging Trends and Technologies

Staying ahead in the dropshipping industry requires adaptability and a willingness to leverage emerging trends and technologies:

Trending Technologies

1. **AI for Customer Insights**: Tools like ChatGPT or Shopify's AI can help you analyze customer behavior, optimize product listings, and provide personalized shopping experiences.
2. **AR/VR Shopping Experiences**: Augmented reality (AR) can let customers visualize products in their environment, especially in niches like home décor or fashion.
3. **Voice Commerce**: With the rise of smart assistants like Alexa and Google Assistant, optimize your store for voice search.

Upcoming Trends

- **Personalization**: Tailor recommendations and marketing messages to individual customer preferences.
- **Sustainability**: Eco-friendly products and sustainable business practices are becoming increasingly important to consumers.
- **Community Building**: Brands that create a sense of community, such as through forums or social media groups, foster loyalty and engagement.

Summary Checklist

Before launching your dropshipping business, ensure you've addressed the following:

1. Identified a profitable and sustainable niche.
2. Researched demand and competition using tools like Google Trends and Audience Insights.
3. Tested products and validated the niche through small-scale campaigns.
4. Established a strong brand and online presence.
5. Implemented digital marketing strategies to drive traffic and sales.
6. Focused on customer retention through loyalty programs and exceptional service.
7. Optimized operations for efficiency and scalability.
8. Explored opportunities for global expansion.
9. Leveraged emerging technologies and industry trends.

By following this comprehensive guide, you'll be equipped to find and dominate a dropshipping niche while building a sustainable and profitable business.

www.ingramcontent.com/pod-product-compliance
Lightning Source LLC
Chambersburg PA
CBHW062115220526
45471CB00010B/3744